A SAMPLER
OF ALPHABETS

Published in 1987 by Sterling Publishing Co., Inc.
Two Park Avenue, New York, NY 10016

English translation © 1987 Sterling Publishing Co., Inc.

© 1984 Modes et Travaux

First published in France under the title *Le Livre des Abecedaires*

A Sterling/Lark Book

Produced by Lark Books
50 College Street, Asheville, NC 28801

Translated from the French by Phyllis Stiles

Illustrations on pages 4 and 5 courtesy of DMC Corporation and of Bernie Wolf

Library of Congress Catalog Card Number: 86-63821

ISBN 0-8069-6508-8 hardcover

ISBN 0-8069-6508-1 paperback

Distributed in Canada by Oak Tree Press Company, Ltd.
c/o Canadian Manda Group, P.O. Box 920, Station U, Toronto, Ontario M8Z 5P9, Canada

Distributed in the United Kingdom by Blandford Press
Link House, West Street, Poole, Dorset BH15 1LL, England

Distributed in Australia by Capricorn Ltd.
P.O. Box 665, Lane Cove, New South Wales 2066, Australia

Printed in Hong Kong by South China Printing Company

A SAMPLER
OF ALPHABETS

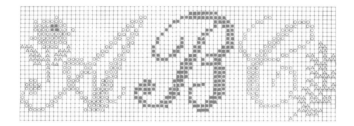

MODES & TRAVAUX

A Sterling/Lark Book

 Sterling Publishing Co., Inc., New York

*Many different stitches can be used in sampler
work. There are a number of books
devoted to embroidery and needlepoint stitches
in which you will find thorough instructions
for dozens of different ones. To help you begin
creating your own beautiful sampler, we've shown
just a few of the simple, basic stitches here.*

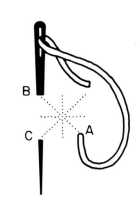

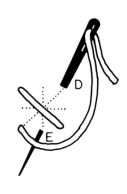

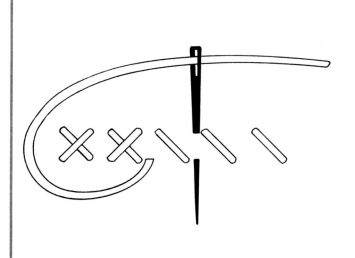

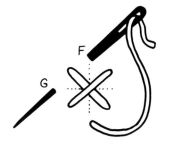

CROSS STITCH

Cross stitch is worked over an even number of vertical
and horizontal threads so that each finished stitch fills
a square. To work it in rows, bring thread to right side
of fabric at lower right, insert needle at upper left.
Continue working these half crosses to the end of the
row (if you're working a sampler in half cross stitch,
this step completes a row). Then, working along the
row in the other direction, bring needle out at lower
left and insert at upper right to complete the crosses.
The upper thread of all crosses should lie in the same
direction to give a uniform look to the work.

DOUBLE CROSS STITCH

This is a cross stitch which is crossed again. It is worked over an
even number of horizontal and vertical threads. Bring needle out
to right side and take a diagonal stitch. Bring needle out directly
below end of stitch and take another diagonal stitch across center
of first diagonal. Bring needle out at midpoint between two lower
points of star, and cross center. Complete the star by bringing
needle out at side midpoint, then crossing center. The result
should be a star contained in a perfect square.

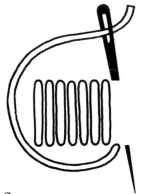
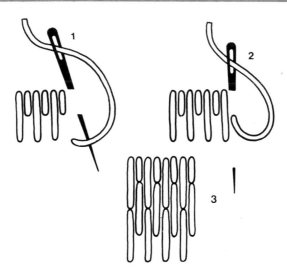
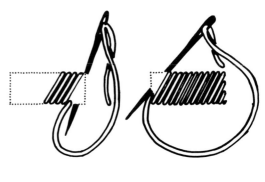

SATIN STITCH

Begin by bringing needle out at lower side of band to be covered. Insert needle directly above that point and pull thread through. Work next stitch beside first, beginning at lower side of design band. An even satin stitch will be achieved by using a stabbing motion with the needle rather than going from one side of the band to the other in a continuous motion. Take care to make a good edge and not to make stitches too long.

LONG AND SHORT SATIN STITCH

Before beginning, determine the direction stitches will take within a given shape. The direction of the long and short satin stitch is of prime importance, since the flat field it produces will reflect light accordingly. In the first row, alternate long and short stitches along the perimeter of the area to be filled. In subsequent rows, work long stitches, always piercing the end of the stitch above. Fill in the last row with short satin stitches.

SLANTED SATIN STITCH

This is a good stitch for working curved bands of embroidery, such as letters and numbers. First establish the angle of the slant by taking an initial stitch where it will be the full width of the design band. Then work outward along the band. When work in that direction is complete, return to the point of the beginning stitch and work outward in the other direction. To prevent flattening the angle, take care to insert the needle exactly next to the preceding stitch at upper edge of band and slightly away from preceding stitch at lower edge of band.

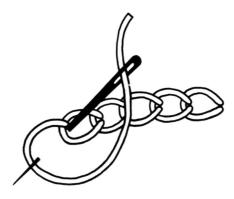
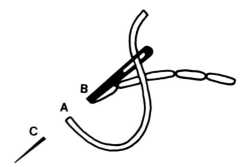

STEM STITCH

Outline with this stitch, or use it to cover lines within a design. Working along a line, bring needle out to right side. Insert needle along line to right, then bring needle back out half a stitch length back. For a wider stitch, angle the needle slightly. Shorten the stitches at curves.

CHAIN STITCH

The chain stitch is useful both for outlining and for filling. Bring thread to right side along the line to be covered, and hold down with left thumb. Insert needle where it last exited and bring point out a short distance away along line, with thread under tip of needle. Continue, always keeping the working thread beneath needle tip.

BACK STITCH

The back stitch is used as a basis for many other stitches; it also works well as an outline stitch. Bring needle to right side along design line, take a small stitch backward along line, and bring needle to right side again in front of first stitch a stitch length away. Continue along the design line, always finishing stitch by inserting needle at point where last stitch began. The same number of threads should be covered by each stitch.

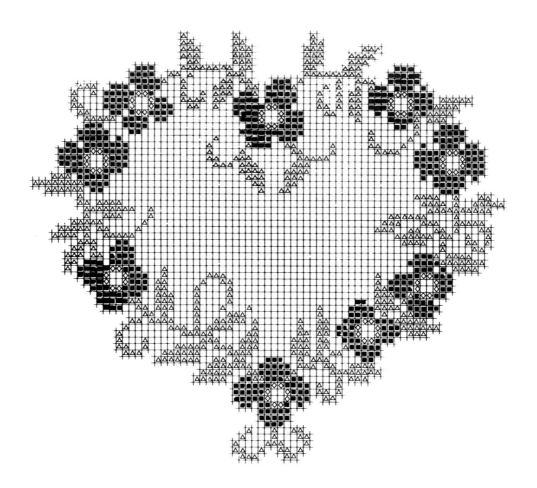

This book is the offspring of the entire team at *Modes et Travaux* magazine in Paris. Here, in a few words, is the story of its birth. *Dominique Roche* had the idea. One day, just by chance, she met an antique sampler and fell in love with it. She began to speak passionately of it. *Pierre Roux* came to share her enthusiasm. He covered Paris looking for additional samplers, and enlisted the help of his family and friends in the search. They scoured France, the Basque region (la Navarre), and even Monaco to uncover these treasures. *Alberto Mantovani* took the book in hand. It is he who presents the book to you in its present form. *Jean-Luc Scotto*, photographer, and *Monique Duveau*, framer, worked miracles to restore each piece, from the best to the most tattered. *Jean-Jacques Ducourtial* coordinated and kept watch over the printing of this lovely book. And I . . . *Hélène Caure*, I wrote all the copy. All this took us, naturally, about nine months. I can honestly say to you that this book is our precious child.

"Black A, white E, red I, green U, and blue O: vowels,
I will someday recite your latent birth . . ."

Just simple letters, simple vowels, with the ability to inspire a poem. This one was written by French poet Arthur Rimbaud in 1871 and is celebrated today. Was he recalling a colorful alphabet which he had mumbled his way through while learning to read? Maybe he was, as other children of his time did. Students labored, too, with their penmanship, taking care with downstrokes and upstrokes, practicing first the straight strokes, then the letters.

From senseless letters come an alphabet of sounds. What differentiates a straightforward alphabet from a sampler alphabet? Whimsy, symbols, little stories, nursery rhymes, illustrations, the embroidered motifs which illuminate the letters and lend them life.

This is what happened with embroidery. Young girls were obliged to learn to sew, to embroider. The sewing lessons were perhaps not happy occasions, yet in them a little girl could let her imagination run rampant. Long live fantasy!

No sampler is the same. Each has its own character.

A beautiful collection, in which the pieces are almost exclusively French, is revealed to you in this book. Let yourself go! Copy any design you like, or create your own dream, taking inspiration from the ingenuity of these young girls and women. The close-up photos allow you to copy or restitch whatever you like.

Under the reign of Queen Victoria, children's literature in England became more imaginative. In France, creativity is apparent in the letters of the alphabet, as can be seen in the beautiful samplers from that era. The creativity is astonishing. Each letter evokes an object, a fruit, a flower, or an animal whose name begins with that letter. In later years, embroiderers seemed happy simply to line letters up in rows and then decorate the border.

Hence, an alphabet sampler was made as the embroiderer pleased. Many of these are signed and dated. They have been hidden away and discovered in the hands of junk shop owners, antique

collectors, or at flea markets. Quite often the frames were in worse condition than the fabric. Many samplers had to be reframed in order to conserve and protect them.

Certain kinds of frames were stylish during the late 19th and early 20th century: English style threaded pitch pine (of reddish colored wood), Napoleon III's black and gold wood, common cane (certainly the least expensive), Empire style black wood, and gilded frames, cast in plaster, then regilded.

Patterns for six original sampler designs are provided for you at the end of this book. The counted thread designs are graphed for use on canvas and other even-weave fabrics. The outline designs can be used with canvas, or for free-style embroidery. Now you may, at your leisure, begin your own sampler collection by patiently "pulling the needle."

This delightful composition abounds with color on fine white canvas. Two alphabets, one small and the other in old English capitals. The Roman numerals are unusual in sampler work. The interest is in the decorative motifs and the pretty floral frame. Two wreaths of mixed flowers are worked in studied colors, and the geometric design is reminiscent of a snowflake. The name in the signature, Palmyre Lefèvre, stirs romantic dreams. The sampler was made in 1905 and worked in half cross stitch.

13

Marie Borondée

Arzew 28 Juillet 1903

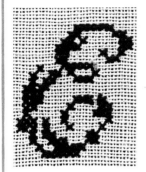 xtraordinary precision is rare and
certainly deserves admiration. Two alphabets are neatly worked in cross
stitch on fine canvas: one red in italic capital letters, a second mauve in
block letters adorned with yellow flowers and green leaves. A double
border covers the perimeter. Tiny motifs act as signets. The signature,
location, and date finish the work.

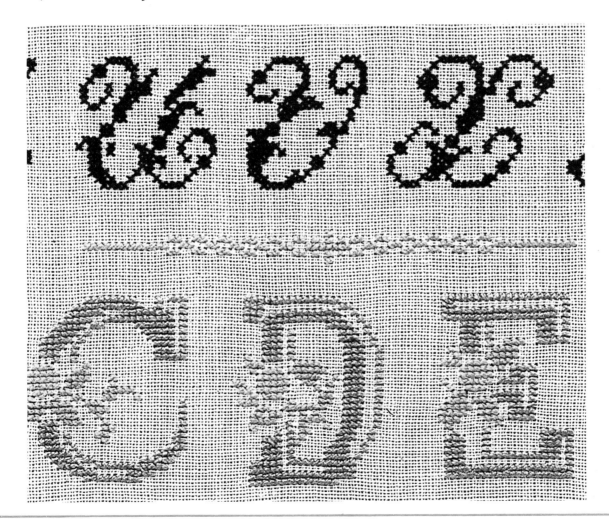

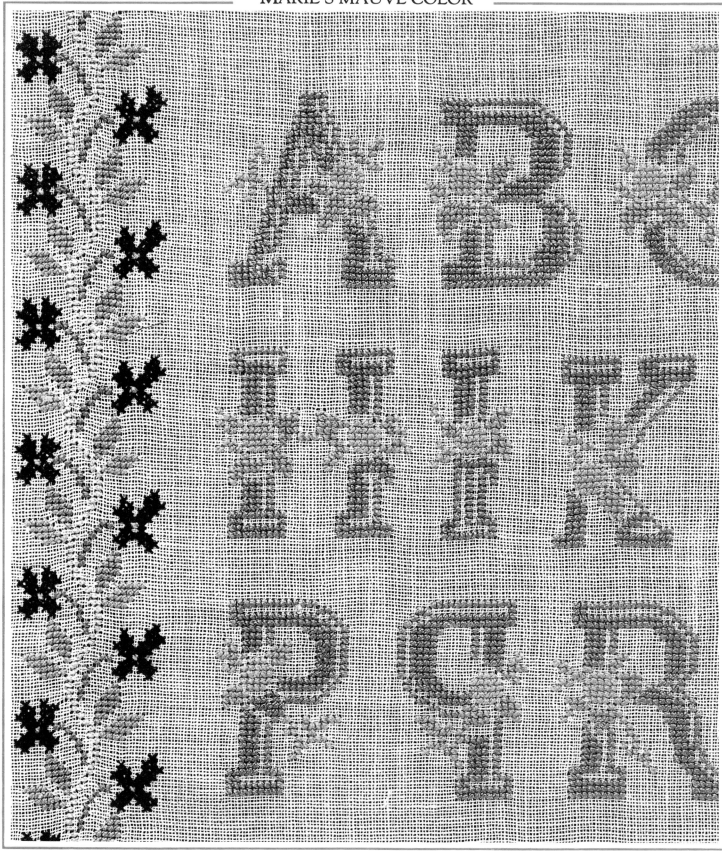

Delightful . . . and rare! These two antique cross stitch samplers are from Clamecy, France. Both are dated, and they were made 21 years apart. The one dated 1860, on etamine, is composed of an alphabet, numbers, the first and last names. It is unusual in that it contains the embroiderer's address. The more recent (and still over 100 years old!) sampler was worked on linen by an 11-year-old girl, and features alphabets, numbers, a bird, and very simple ornamental motifs.

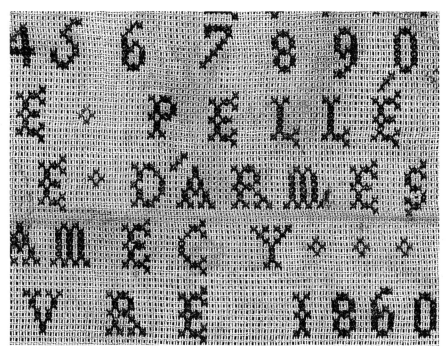

18

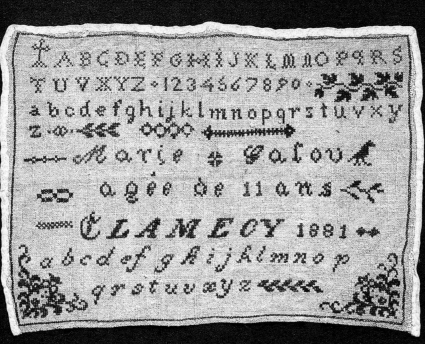

19

eaturing
outstanding workmanship, 12-year-old
Joséphine Marsot's cross stitch sampler is
adorned with three alphabets, a basket of
pansies, two goblets filled with flowers, trees,
and borders. Ravishing colors are harmoniously
realized on a background of white canvas. It
dates from the last century.

21

he man on a bicycle is quite a picture from the past! The ornate alphabet is worked in green and rose; the signature, location, and year are in red. The dog and chicken convey a wonderful sense of motion, and a tidy garland of leaves serves as a border. This heartfelt piece is worked in cross stitch on white canvas.

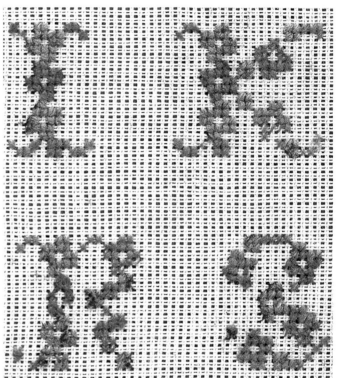

DOE AND STAG

nquestionably a masterpiece, this original and meticulous cross stitch work! Dense and flowery letters are beautifully worked in three colors on white canvas. The frame is rich and elaborate without being heavy. At the central point are the doe and stag, surrounded by some favorite woods creatures. The embroiderer's name and date are neatly placed along the bottom.

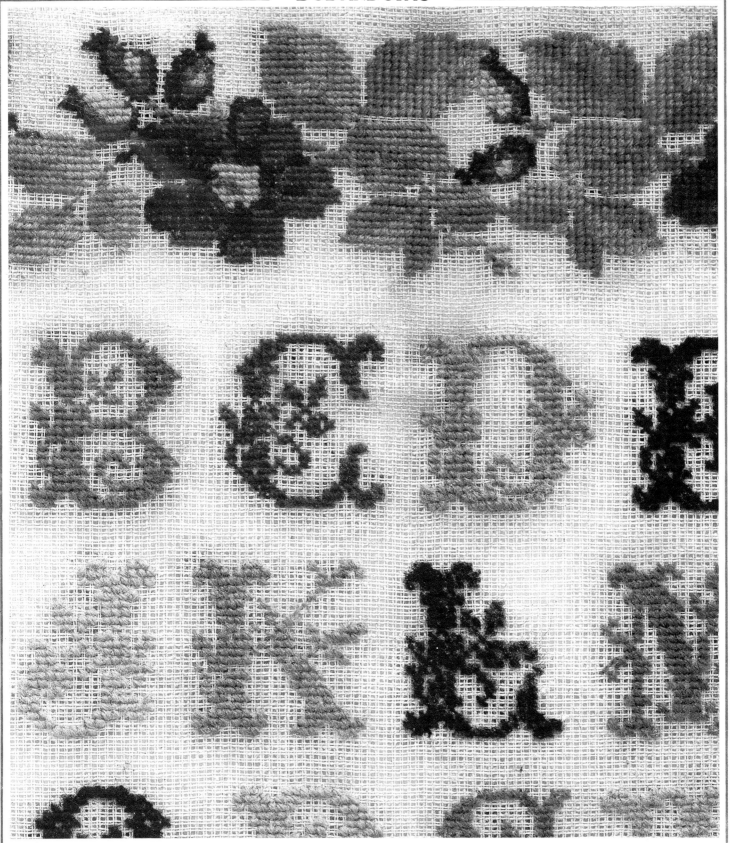

olorful and delicate, this sampler is a nicely balanced composition on canvas. Three colors are used for the alphabet. Two splendid initials are intertwined and centered among flowers and a magnificent butterfly. An elegant signature, in italics, is worked in two colors. A border on each side and a flower at each corner complete this very pretty cross stitch work.

34

eligious and secular themes are intermixed. The alphabet and numbers are in one color, surrounded by a lovely border of flowers. Religious and holy symbols are used—but a handsome cat as well. Birds, fish, a dog, two orange trees, and a child display excellent craftsmanship in cross stitch. A 10-year-old girl worked this sampler in 1898.

abcdefghijklmnopqrstuvxyz

Eugénie Marchand

ABCDEFGHIJKLMNO

STUVWXYZ·123456

ABCDEFGHIJKLMNOPQRST

ABCDEFGHIJ

MNOPQRSTUV

XYZ·1234567890·PA

souvenir

antalizing and cheerful, this piece is cross stitched on white canvas with red cotton floss. An alphabet of lower case letters and the date, 1895, precede the first and last names of the embroiderer. The signature is emphasized by its position, centered and flanked by two stars. Eugénie Marchand apparently loved her work! The place is precisely stated Paris and the word souvenir leaves us dreaming. Detailed corners ornament a simple framing border.

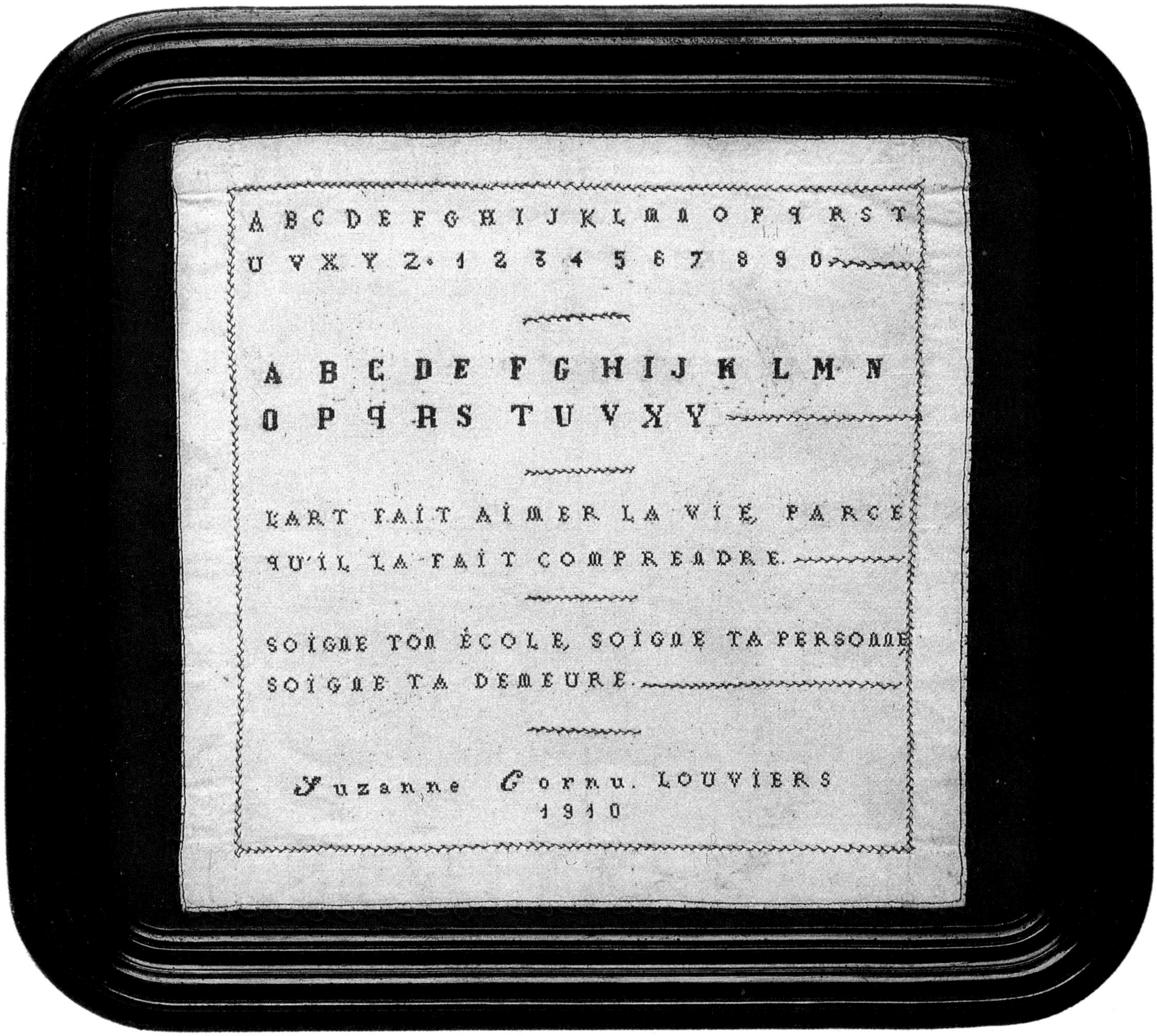
A B C D E F G H I J K L M N O P Q R S T
U V X Y Z. 1 2 3 4 5 6 7 8 9 0.
A B C D E F G H I J K L M N
O P Q R S T U V X Y
L'ART FAÎT AÎMER LA VÎE, PARCE
QU'ÎL LA FAÎT COMPRENDRE.
SOÎGNE TON ÉCOLE, SOÎGNE TA PERSONNE
SOÎGNE TA DEMEURE.
Suzanne Cornu. LOUVÎERS
1910

Distinguished letters
and meaningful words. Very fine cross stitch is worked in red floss on white
linen, the piece is hemstitched and edged in picot. This student offers two
thoughts to ponder: Art causes one to love life because it imparts
understanding of life. Take care of your school, take care of your
appearance, take care of your home.

umptuous!
*Four alphabets in cross stitch are
perfectly placed on this white canvas. Four generous motifs, superb
in form and color, embellish the
corners. A religious inspiration—
the cross and sacred initials—set
off to the left. In addition, a rich
bouquet is centered at the top and
a sentimental dedication, To
Mama, at the bottom. It is neither
signed nor dated, what a pity!*

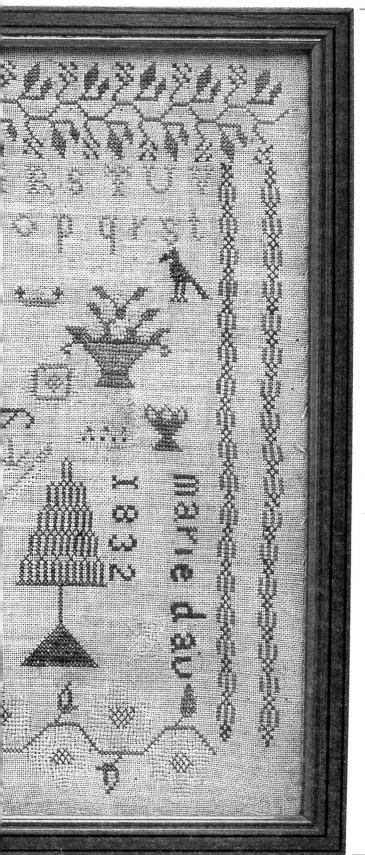

ross stitched on linen, this 1832 sampler is the oldest piece in our collection. Religious motifs—the altar tabernacle, cross, and candles—are set among floral and animal motifs. Tiny leaves and flowers make up the border. The colors have faded, but the airy effect is preserved. Two alphabets, one upper case and one lower, are neatly worked across the top of the piece. The signature and date are still readable.

ust one alphabet, but in a rainbow of colors. This 13-year-old girl expressed herself through the motifs she worked in delicate half cross stitch. A pretty bouquet, birds, and kittens encircle a variety of symbols. Do they represent religion? Justice? Play? Work? A neat border serves as a frame.

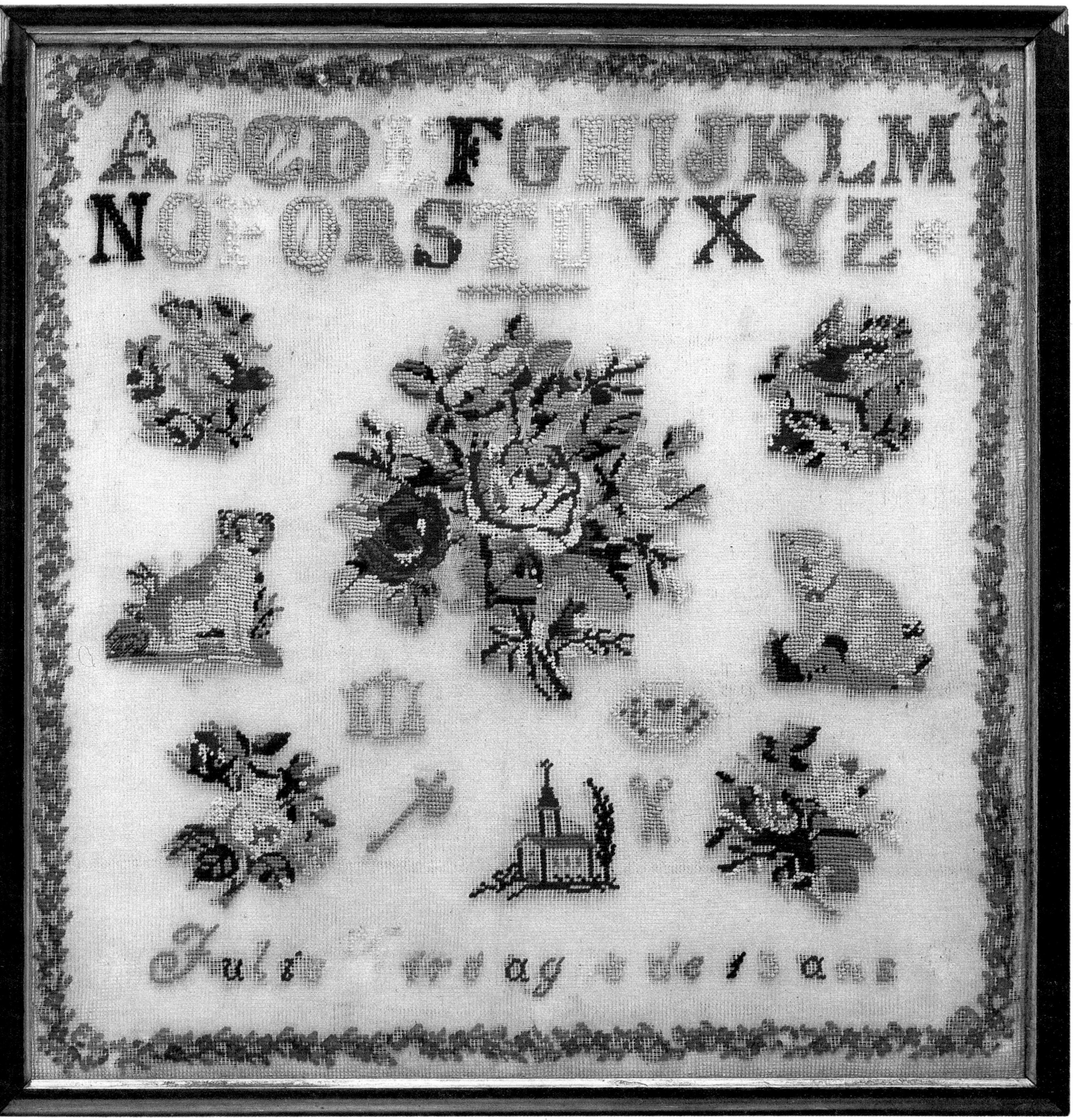
ABCDEFGHIJKLM
NOPQRSTUVXYZ

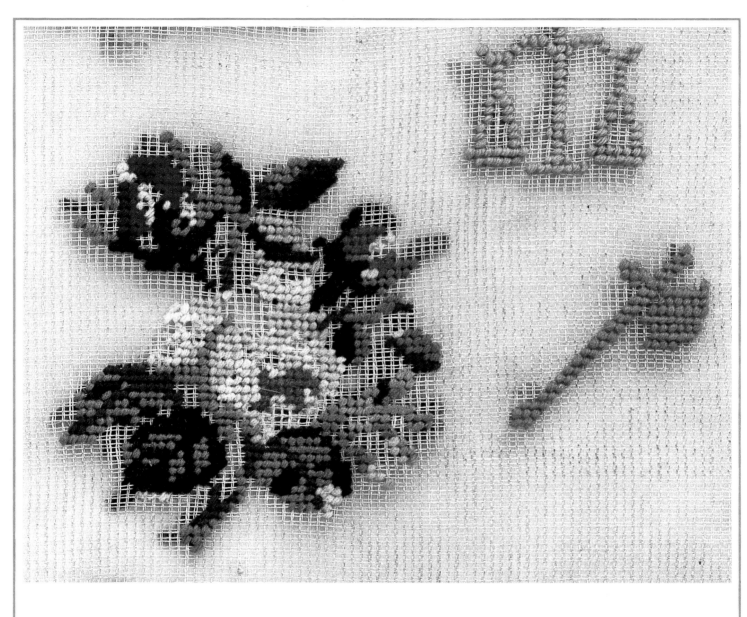

his bright and cheery *souvenir d'ecole is worked in cross stitch. A sedate blue alphabet and an elegant red one are neatly stitched on canvas that probably once was white. Two pairs of motifs decorate the corners. The vertical borders feature small flowers, the horizontal ones show trios of carnations. A signature, an occasion, a place, and a date: a perfect piece, everything is here.*

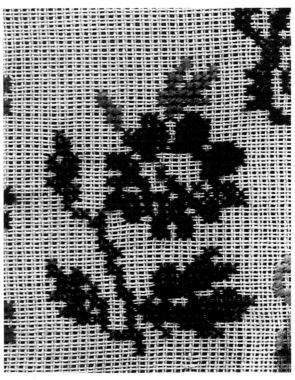

he two signatures indicate this stately sampler might be the work of four hands. It features a very elegant alphabet in soft tones, and is worked in half cross stitch on tan canvas. A bird of paradise on a branch, people in 17th-century costumes, roses in full bloom, all are contained within a lovely floral border. Unfortunately, there is no date.

eautiful craftsmanship and balanced composition highlight this spirited piece. Upper case letters in three styles are worked in red cross stitch on white canvas. The borders are in pairs, one a Greek design and one a zigzag line. Two small birds facing each other serve as a signature. This is undoubtedly the work of a student.

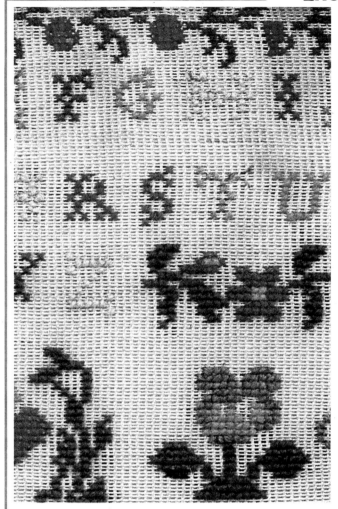

 single alphabet and a great deal of imagination. A variety of odd motifs are symmetrically placed around the cross—flowers, two exotic birds, and bowls of fruit. The border of small roses is very pretty. Charming colors are used, and several different kinds of thread. Although it is neither signed nor dated, the innocence and originality of this cross-stitched composition brings to mind the work of a child.

69

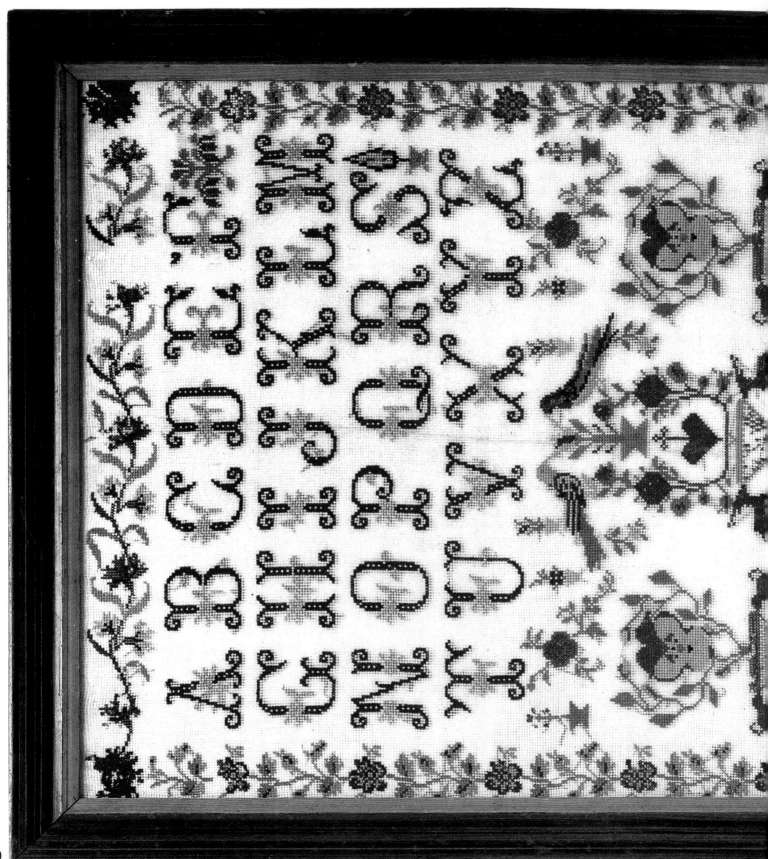

elightful flowers everywhere! Both bright and subtle colors were used for this cross stitch embroidery on white canvas. The well-balanced floral motifs are undoubtedly symbolic: they seem to convey very personal thoughts. Pretty birds rest beside a sacred heart suspended from a cross. The floral border is magnificent. Concluding the work are a location, date and a signature (Eugénie was a very popular first name in France at the turn of the century, but now is rarely heard).

ABCDEFGHIJKLMNOPQRSTUVW
1 2 3 4 5 6 7 8 9 0 11 12 13 14 15 16 17 1
ABCDEFGHIJKLMNPQRST
WXYZ 1 2 3 4 5 6 7 8 9 0
A B C D E F G H I J K L M N O
G T U V W X Y Z
ABCDEFGHIJKLMNOP
S T U V W X Y Z
ABCDEFJHIJKLM
OPQRSTUVXYZ
ABCDEFGHIJKLM
TQRSTUVXYZ
RENÉE LELIÈVRE
LIEUREY

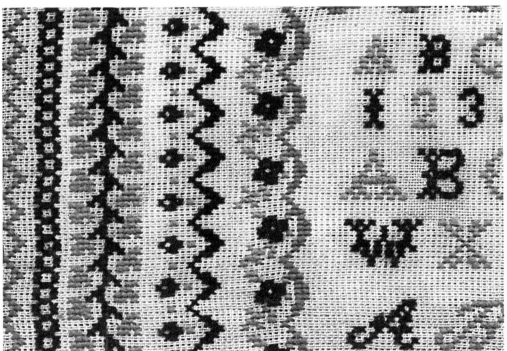

Decorative numbers and letters in red and green cross stitch are worked on white canvas. A selection of borders frame the work, and the small repetitive motifs provide symmetry. The embroiderer's name and the location are nicely stitched, but no date is given.

76

*E*specially charming and simple, this ribbon-wrapped sampler is worked in half cross stitch on natural-colored canvas. It is neither signed nor dated. The alphabet is arranged in vertical columns that read from left to right. A boat and a sailor, primitive in design, float alongside the house. An unusual border adorns the two sides. A candle and candlestick, a glass, and dainty flowers . . . such imagination!

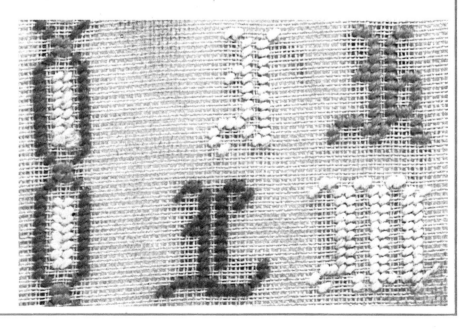

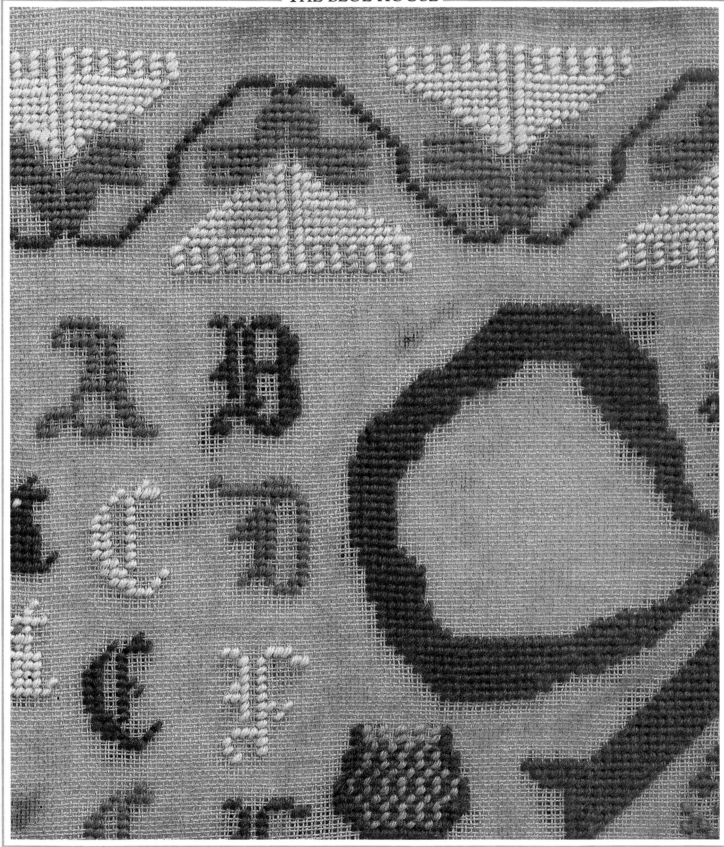

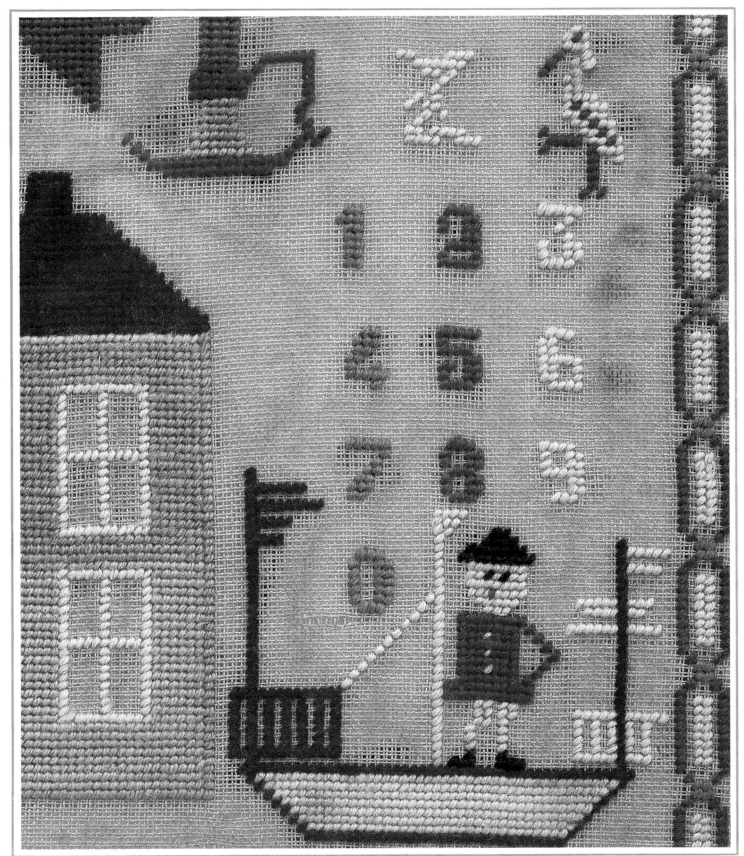

nique in its use of so much black, this alphabet sampler features three majestic alphabets of capital letters, worked in cross stitch on white canvas. Floral motifs and geometric designs are framed by a delicate border of flowers. A wreath of roses and rose buds emphasizes the central motif, a young girl in a country setting. The work is signed and dated.

Unusual in its oblong format, this piece is cross stitched on canvas which originally was white. Three alphabets and some numbers are worked in bright colors, and are adorned with just two motifs. It is unclear whether the letters at the bottom have any significance, but the pink M appears unbalanced. The date is very visible because of its density and strong color.

84

86

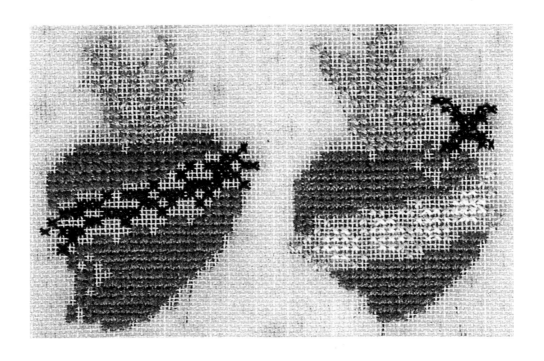

*U*nsophisticated and quite pious, this small sampler includes a single alphabet worked in cross stitch in two colors on mono canvas. The symbolic hearts of Mary and Christ are centered between two chalices of fruit. A border of flowers frames the piece and continues the color scheme. The first name in the signature, Malvina, appears to be Italian, but the last name, Roisset, is assuredly French. It is dated 1891.

his cross stitch
sampler was Eugénie's classroom project. One can sense the effort
the little girl put into her embroidery, worked in red cross stitch on
large-weave white canvas. The teacher must have been quite
strict. . . . It is framed in a square, signed with
a first name only, and dated 1931.

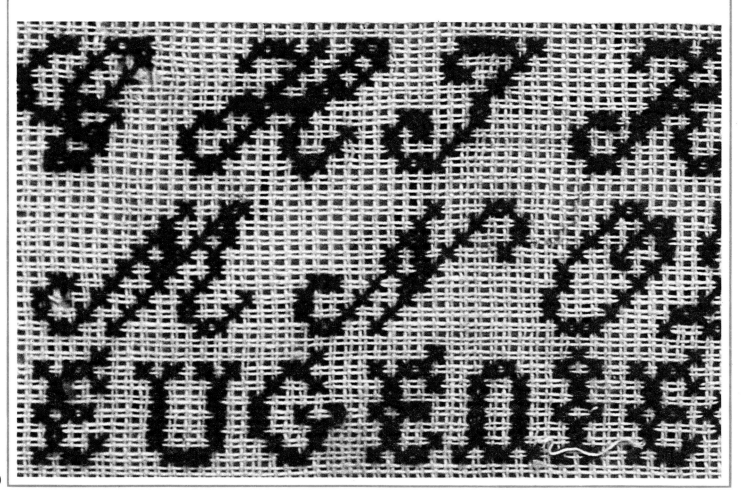

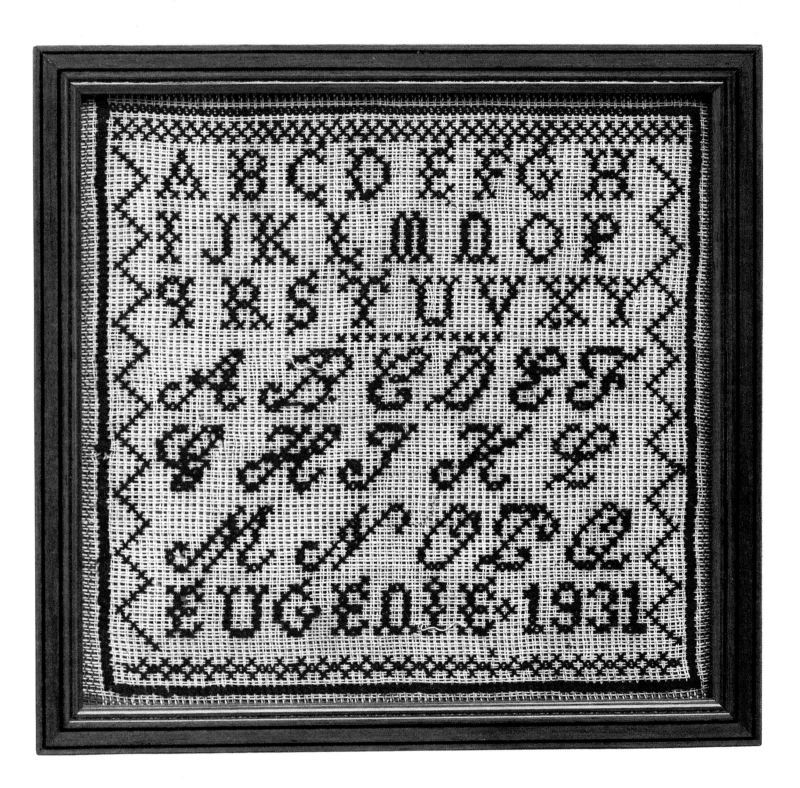

Perhaps an entire school year's work, this sampler features a variety of embroidery stitches—herringbone, backstitch, feather, etc. Borders, alphabets, numbers and darning stitches were added, all worked in red. Red initials, in cross stitch, end the work. The author signs and finishes without fanfare, just the family name and the year 1901.

93

Toys adorn an alphabet of children's designs for the nursery. Soft colors emphasize a balanced composition. Embroidered in Brilliant Embroidery and Cutwork Thread on fine white linen, this design comes from the team at Modes et Travaux. The design, ready to copy, is on page 106.

pdated colors enliven an alphabet that dances around a generous bouquet. A creation of Modes et Travaux, *it is worked in half cross stitch (or petit point) on tan canvas with wool yarn. Four different corner motifs give the design harmony and balance. Graphs for this design are on pages* 112-115.

ainty floral hearts and a colorful alphabet are cross stitched on white canvas with matte cotton. Small motifs are inserted between graceful capital letters. Brightly colored pieces of fruit in the bowl are repeated in the cheery border design. This exclusive from Modes et Travaux *was inspired by old samplers, but adapted to today's style. The graphed pattern for this design is on pages* 108-111.

lean and bold, the single alphabet is crowned with a wreath where birds chirp and butterflies linger. The inspiration is modern, with a slight touch of the past that we love. This elegant sampler is worked in half cross stitch with matte cotton on brown canvas. The graphed pattern for the design, created by Modes et Travaux, is on pages 116-119.

Practically a family history, this sampler features an assortment of original motifs, and a strong alphabet of upper case letters worked in red. It is cross stitched with matte cotton on cream-colored etamine. The airy border appears to be of English origin. The design is by Modes et Travaux, *and the graphed pattern is found on page 120.*

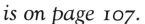

*L*ively embellishments
for a linen dish towel. A graceful script alphabet is embroidered on a
towel of red windowpane checks—a towel and alphabet sampler
combined! A wicker basket overflows with fruit
to lend a feeling of bounty, and dainty wall-
flowers provide a border. It is embroidered in
matte cotton with long and short and satin
stitches. The pattern for this design
is on page 107.

A B C D E F

G H I J K L

M N O P Q R

S T U V W X Y Z

107

109

■ light blue

O red

▲ gold

△ light green

◇ yellow

◆ green

• dark green

111

112

- green
- dark green
- burgundy
- red
- orange
- light orange
- chestnut
- gold

U rust

X deep violet

◆ pale mauve

∧ mauve

★ blue

◇ lavender

● white

— yellow

114

115

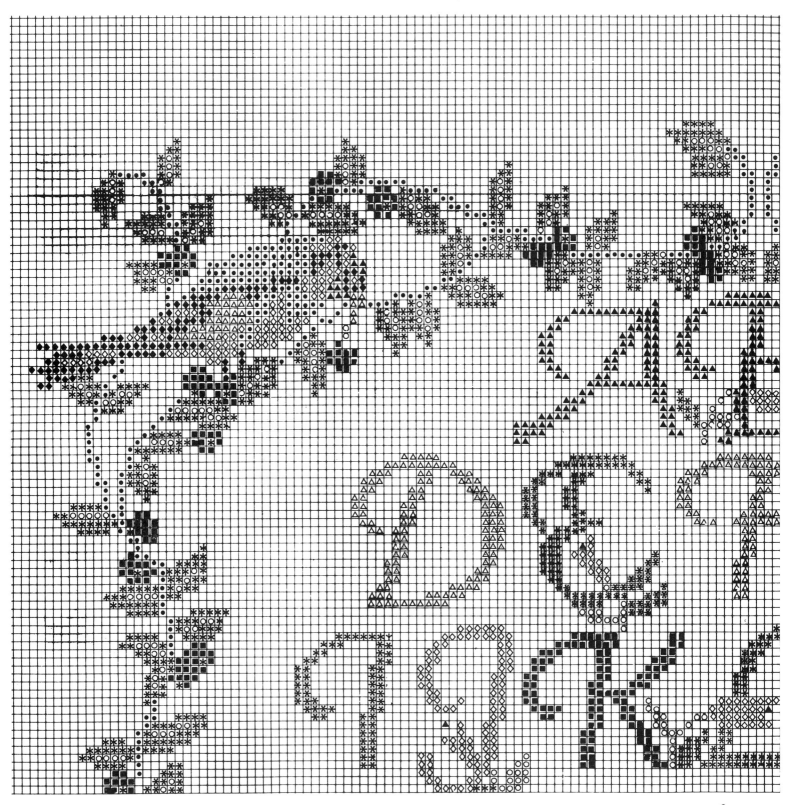

116

◐ light green
■ royal blue
◇ white
◆ black

▲ yellow
▲ red
● gold
✳ dark green

117

119

✗ royal blue
✚ light blue
❱ green
❰ red
● yellow

120